# STARS

## SOLAR SYSTEM

Lynda Sorensen

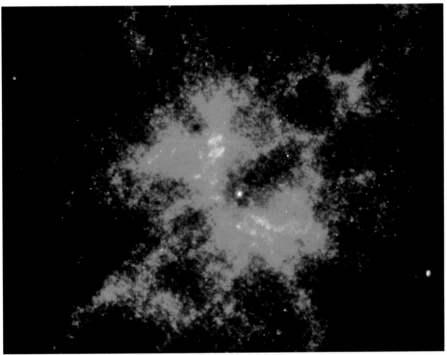

The Rourke Corporation, Inc.
Vero Beach, Florida 32964

Edited by Sandra A. Robinson


PHOTO CREDITS
All photos courtesy NASA except page 7 © Lynn M. Stone


**Library of Congress Cataloging-in-Publication Data**

Sorensen, Lynda, 1953-
    Stars / by Lynda Sorensen.
    p.   cm. — (The Solar system)
    Includes index.
    Summary: Discusses different kinds of stars, including dwarfs
and giants; red, white, and blue stars; shooting stars; the North
Star; and our sun.
    ISBN 0-86593-276-X
    1. Stars—Juvenile literature. [1. Stars.] I. Title. II. Series.
III. Series: Solar system (Vero Beach, Fla.)
QB801.S5  1993
523.8—dc20

                                        93-10475
                                            CIP
                                             AC

# TABLE OF CONTENTS

# THE STARS

Stars are hot, fiery **globe**-shaped masses of gas that produce their own light. The closest star to Earth is the sun.

There are billions of stars in outer space. On a clear night, a star watcher might be able to see as many as four or five thousand.

Stars look like tiny, twinkling points of light because they are so far from Earth. Most stars, however, are huge—as large or larger than the sun.

*Stars are huge, but appear to be tiny, twinkling lights*

# A SPECIAL STAR

The sun is the closest star to Earth—and by far the most important. The sun provides heat and light and a basic source of food.

Plants use sunlight to make food for themselves. All animals, including people, depend upon plants—or animals that eat plants—for their food.

So even though it is 93 million miles away, the sun makes life on Earth possible.

*Green plants change sunlight to food*

# DWARFS AND GIANTS

Scientists group stars by size. Rare megastars, for example, are incredibly large. One megastar is big enough to fill the 93 million miles of space between Earth and the sun!

A second group, giant stars, are far larger than the sun. Most of the stars we see in the sky, including the sun, are called main-sequence stars.

White dwarfs are fairly small stars. Neutron stars are tiny. Some are just 12 miles across!

*Over billions of years, a star may grow to incredible size*

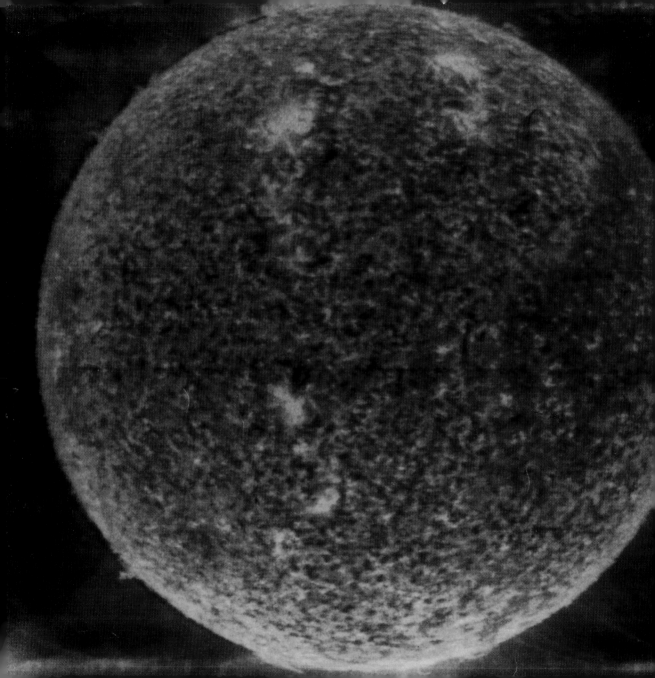

# RED, WHITE AND BLUE STARS

Stars shine with different colors. We cannot see the colors by just gazing at the night sky, but there are yellow, red, white and blue stars.

A star's color depends on the temperature of the star's surface. All stars are hot, but blue stars are the hottest. They have surface temperatures up to 50,000 degrees Fahrenheit! Paper burns at less than 500 degrees.

Yellow stars, like the sun, are cooler than blue or white stars. Red stars are the coolest stars.

*The sun is a yellow star*

*The National Aeronautics and Space Administration's (NASA) powerful infrared telescope on Mauna Kea, Hawaii*

*The IRAS Satellite, launched in 1983 from California, photographed stars and other heavenly objects*

# CONSTELLATIONS

Many stars are in groups called **constellations.** Long ago, star watchers thought stars in constellations formed outlines in the sky of well-known people, animals or objects. One familiar constellation was named Ursa Major (the Great Bear) because the stars appear to form a bear's outline.

Within the Great Bear constellation are seven stars that look like the outline of a cup with a long handle. This group is known as the Big Dipper.

14 *Stars and clouds of gas and dust in the constellation Orion, as photographed through an infrared telescope in space*

# GALAXIES

**Galaxies** are huge groups of billions of stars. Our **solar system**—the sun, planets and moons—and billions of stars make up the Milky Way galaxy. Planet Earth is a tiny speck in the galaxy.

All the stars you see in the night sky are part of the Milky Way. Beyond our galaxy are millions of other galaxies that are incredibly far from Earth.

*A satellite trail streaks across the Milky Way*

# THE NORTH STAR

Before they had ships' instruments to guide them, sailors used the North Star to find their way at sea. The North Star was a good guide because it was always in the same location in the sky.

Because the Earth moves through space, most stars look as if they, too, change their position in the sky. However, the position of the North Star, also known as Polaris, does not change.

Polaris is the brightest star in the constellation Ursa Minor, Little Bear.

*Sailors on ocean voyages used the North Star as a guidepost*

## SHOOTING STARS

A shooting star looks like a candle flame racing through the night sky. However, a shooting "star" is not a star but a **meteor**—a piece of burning rock.

A meteor is first a **meteoroid,** a rock in space. When a meteoroid plunges toward Earth, it heats up and catches fire, becoming a meteor.

Meteors usually burn up before they strike Earth. A large meteor that survives its fall, though, can make a huge hole, or **crater.**

*A meteor, or "shooting star," dashes across the night sky*

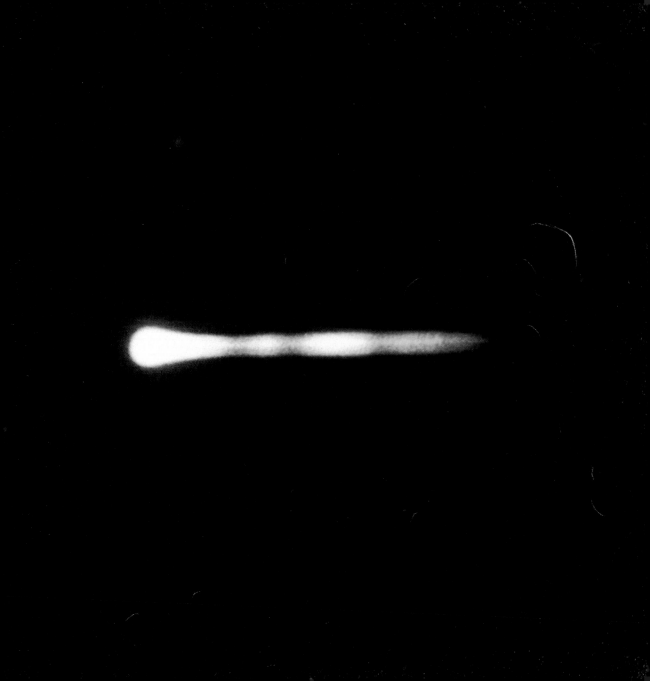

# STUDYING THE STARS

**Astronomy** is the study of the stars and planets. The scientists who study astronomy are called **astronomers.**

Astronomers use telescopes to help them see heavenly bodies more clearly. The glass and mirrors in telescopes make distant objects look close to Earth.

Astronomers work in buildings called **observatories.** Many observatories are open at certain times for everyone to visit.

# Glossary

**astronomer** (uh STRON uh mer) — a scientist who studies the sun, moon, stars and other heavenly bodies

**astronomy** (uh STRON uh mee) — the study of the sun, moon, stars and other heavenly bodies and events

**constellation** (kahn still A shun) — a group of stars whose outline looks like a person, animal or some other well-known object

**crater** (KRA ter) — a pit or dent in the surface of a moon or planet

**galaxy** (GAL ex ee) — a group of billions of stars

**globe** (GLOBE) — round, ball-shaped object

**meteor** (MEET ee er) — a flaming piece of rock from space

**meteoroid** (MEET ee er oid) — a rock in space

**observatory** (uhb ZERV uh tor ee) — a place where astronomers view and study the stars and solar system

**solar system** (SO ler SIS tim) — the sun, planets and other heavenly bodies that revolve around the sun

# INDEX